THESE
DAYS
OF
CANDY

MANUEL
PAUL
LÓPEZ

THESE
DAYS
OF
CANDY

For Kiabra —
Sister in arms. You
are an inspiration
and guiding light.
Lots of luck
on your
journey toward
greatness. Lots of
love,
2018

N͠oMI
PRESS

Published by Noemi Press, Inc. A Nonprofit Literary
Organization.
www.noemipress.org

Cover and Book Design by Steve Halle
Cover Image adapted from *English: Chocolate Candies* by Alek-
sey Pogrebnoj-Alexandroff, licensed under Creative Com-
mons 3.0 (CC BY 3.0).

First Edition
ISBN: 978-1-934819-72-2

This book was published with support from Virginia Tech.

for mandie nicole

for my parents

Dedicado a la memoria de mi abuelita,
Julia Martha López (1927–2017)

CONTENTS

IV

PROLOGUE

Like a fish tinged by the ocean
I walk on sad shoes, weary
wondering land language
wondering demarcation splinter
wondering separation blues
wondering ocean bottom
Like a fish tinged by the ocean
I walk on sad shoes, weary

I

My heart is the shyest object in the world.
—Frank Lima

THE DAY OF A STENOGRAPHER

1

A stenographer ought to regulate his life.

Here is the exact timetable of my daily life:

Get up: 5:35 AM; bewildered: from 6 AM to 11:30 AM

Eat lunch: 12 PM. Eat only foods that resemble interplanetary forms wedded in genuflection.

Examine shadows throughout the day.

Carry thermometer in breast pocket that bears all and consumes all.

From 1–2:25 PM subscribe to hundreds of tabloids from around the world and cancel every last one of them the very next day.

Walk from 2:30–3:30 PM and daydream a rigorous Bobby Desnos poem while embracing a harrowing fear of all sense of self—my ballpoint is incredibly impressionable.

3:32–4:28 PM fast and dine on the clarity to which hunger can only give rise.

4:30-6:28 PM remain intemperate in the halls of memory that thump their sick song while stenographing a fevered description of a sun burnishing the last gasp of day.

Eat dinner standing on one leg: my food must be shelled, re-shelled then shelled again, using everyday household affixers, a process repeated ad nauseam until there is nothing visibly left of the organism but a ball of tape, thumbtacks, thread and various coats of glue.

This is a performance of small-scale wreckage.

This is an elegy for environmental heartbreak.

A stenographer must be a seasoned performance artist.

A stenographer must toil without fear regardless of what's at stake.

After dinner another walk: it must never exceed 2,011 steps because the Maya should never be mocked.

Read late into the evening, something delicious like alurista's *Et Tú...Raza*

Sleep at an undisclosed time and listen to Satie.

2

Our shadows speak.

Our shadows conspire with cathedrals in the sky.

Our shadows paint intricate murals with wild hands and glass spinnerets.

Our shadows are full-grown water barrels left to fairytale giants with grass slippers to drink from.

Thoreau is a shadow.

The shadowed cathedral is a transmutation of early twentieth century jazz musicians.

Frida is a shadow.

When I measured my heart it weighed 368 kilograms.

I stenographed *No!* but the world did not listen. The cardiologist did not listen.

I threatened my pericardium with a hand shovel if it didn't drop weight.

By nightfall, I was heartless.

By nightfall, I was a shadow's shadow.

In my dreams I stenographed a shaky manifesto of solitude and isolation, the shadow's shadow song.

3

"Who do you stenograph for?" the old stenographer asked the young stenographer.

"Who do I stenograph for? I stenograph for the public record," the young stenographer responded. "Isn't that our purpose? I mean, who do you stenograph for," he asked.

"I stenograph for god," the old stenographer answered.

The young stenographer dropped his shoulders and mumbled something about better to become a poet as he walked away into the night shaking his head.

4

You're a real imagination. That's what your grandmother always said, a real imagination, mijito. Now keep

stenographing your big heart away because the world
needs to change with beauty in mind.

5

The stenographer transcribed a wild man with lots of hair
who thought writing an entire novel without using the let-
ter e would amuse his future selves.

In response, the stenographer laughed at the challenge
and stenographed the entire trial without using the letters
O and J.

Many blame the release of the defendant on this particu-
larly shortsighted and sloppy artistic constraint.

6

Use your stenography to embody everything you can think of,
your tío urged. He said, Even if it's fundamentally wrong—do
it, do it, because it's your freedom as a stenographer to do it!

But what will people think of me, tío?

People won't think anything of you, because your percep-
tions are shitty and unfathomably opaque. Believe me,
mijo, the harm or damage you'd possibly cause is minimal
at best. Me, on the other hand, I'm a different story entire-
ly, My Boy.

7

In court the stenographer is an unwavering crime capsule.

In court the stenographer is an oncologist hemorrhaging ears.

In court the stenographer is a rascal-satirist bricklaying incendiary counts against the state in the name of stenography.

HALLELUJAH MAMA

If you happen to look in the mirror and see a Muppet, close your eyes and clap your hands as hard as you possibly can. This might very well frighten it away. But if you look in the mirror and still see that Muppet staring back at you, chances are you are a Muppet, and that you were always a Muppet.

In the mirror obsess over the dark rings around your Muppet eyes that are a result of the agonizing nights lying in bed awake, contemplating the anonymous Muppet's existence. And the paunch plastered across your midsection now puffed by years of ingesting pints of stout night after night you've brought the sea to a small town in the middle of the desert where everyone around you takes turns drowning.

In the mirror your Muppet eyes reveal something peculiar, a shortcoming you've never quite observed. The universe is problematic, so you hide. You've remained small, hidden and unnoticed like the silver tooth filling in dead uncle Muppet's mouth.

Many close to you have considered you the embodiment of a Muppet severely lacking any recognizable ambitions, so you've endured this life, like an unneeded appendage, like a phantom limb.

In Muppet high school you were an outsider who could play a few bars on the trombone. The blues were always your favorite, but the marches aroused too much anxiety, so you set the instrument down and never played again the dirges you so wanted to reclaim.

You think of your mother a lot these days and the hours she spent teaching you prayers devoted to a Muppet god. The calm you felt when you recited the words, the instantaneous peace that washed over your entire being as you both voiced a ribbon of language affirming Muppet peace, Muppet love, Muppet health. You remember your Muppet heart then, and the way it filled with a buoyant devotion that made you rise.

You often dream of a lamb feeding alone in a vast, empty stadium with a bouquet of geraniums sticking out of its ass. Who knows what this means, but it seems fitting for a Muppet's pun at the end of the day.

We're all lambs, you say, when we're finally jettisoned from the almighty Muppet industry.

CHALK AND INTERSECTION

Lulu drew an intersection in her living room with chalk.

At least that's what you think.

I often wonder why Lulu insists on directing traffic.

She's not even good at it.

She ripped out the carpet one day despite her family's hollering.

Everyone knows when Lulu gets something in that head of hers there's no turning back Lulu.

That's what we love and fear most about Lulu.

"An intersection is a point of space that conjoins several possibilities at once."

And Lulu?

"Collisions are the markings of time exhaling."

Lulu, draw me crosswalks.

Lulu spell STOP.

Inside the O Lulu drew a happy face. Then a sad sad face.

O inspired a confused face.

Irony is what the pilgrims say. And if the pilgrims didn't
say it, Lulu says they certainly should have.

Lulu stresses tragic irony.

Lulu also draws mist. And Lulu draws a mist man. And a
holy mist creator that lurks behind a television set.

Nervous shadows with all this noise and all this time to do
what they want to do.

And what they please to do is make mist, says Lulu.

Lulu discovered early in life she needed to direct traffic to
save herself.

Lulu also discovered in order to achieve this she needed a
uniform and a whistle.

For Christmas Lulu asked her family for white gloves but they were too angry and ignored Christmas that year altogether.

Lulu is a gloveless crossing guard.

Lulu is a crossing guard goddess.

On occasion Lulu will shout Danger, Danger, Ima Danger Ranger—

This happens when her family travels at chaotic speeds.

This happens when road rage seethes from her father's eyes.

Last week Lulu couldn't bear the traffic in her apartment so she sat cross-legged in the middle of the intersection, covered her ears and screamed into a whistle.

Her whistle sounded like a pathetic who-who from a sad rain uniform.

This is why most believe she is not very good at directing traffic.

Though I.

You are not very good at directing traffic, said the collision course. Said the carcass mince with fly droppings.

Though I.

Lulu's intersection is designed with birds, trees, and chin-chilla faces in many-colored chalks—

Though her glyphs are fading these days. These days they're fading. These days of candy are fading.

Horray for Lulu!

Lulu's intersection is one that unites destruction and birth.

Beliefs exist even when no one in the room believes the belief.

Lulu is quite an artist.

Quite a quiet artist.

She grits her teeth and art is made.

Lulu's teachers always mentioned these particulars when describing Lulu.

Lulu's her name.

Lulu drew the Svalbard Global Seed Vault and slept in its embraces for two weeks.

Lulu sleeps in her intersection.

Hooray for life, Lulu!

Hooray for Lulu!

THE ONLOOKERS REPORTED:

The boy with an apple on his head clutched his stomach then fell from what seemed like an exhaustion precipitated by hunger.

The coroner's official cause of death:

No one had ever bothered to tell the boy that there was an apple on top of his head.

THE WARRIORS

They stood up to pledge their allegiances to a microwave-able peace option while bathing in a momentary moratori-um on death certificates. With the tickertape cued, the war was over, the war was over. In response they tossed fistfuls of glitter across their barracks and watched it stick to every-thing and everyone as if a future reminder *to be*, to really *be*.

They slept in due to a heavy night of designing elaborate scrapbooks documenting their wanderings around the Tijuana estuary. Absent from the war, the war paused, as their families bookmarked their favorite spots and laughed and ahh-ed at the whole cute of it.

They claimed they forgot their watches and flashlights; they argued they misplaced their nightsticks somewhere in the rec hall; they insisted *that's* why they were late for war, and *that's* why the night was dim.

They slept in and missed the war after dreaming of a very strange man in a very strange outfit who operated a strange, strange factory. "The dream lasted FOREVER," they plead, "and that's why we couldn't hear the alarm.

Ah, Sergeant Beefheart, it's as if our heads melted into our pillows and everything remained sugary."

A platoon of them climbed a flagpole and suddenly there was a tree that offered shade.

They forgot their weapons in the Natural History Museum on a field trip to consider and discuss the evolution of the pentadactylic biped. Onboard, and with the bus gunned to return to a base two hundred and eighty miles away, the museum's director ran after them with a clipboard in hand. She insisted that they retrieve their weapons immediately, that the Natural History Museum no longer issued space for military history.

In the frenzy, a young private rose from her bench at the front of the bus, slid down a window, and saluted the tall, lean director, responding as respectfully as one could under such incalculable conditions, that the stern museum director should rest assured that this humble private wasn't about to become someone's natural history either, so the unfortunate but necessary influx of semi-automatic weapons were going to have to stay, "they are going to have to stay, mam!"

Snip snip snip sounded the scissors in their hands that scissored to pieces the declarations of war.

They were too hip for war, so they stayed up all night drinking tea and reading books by Will Alexander.

They ate pizza and enjoyed Godfathers' I, II, and III in succession. All night long they recited a whirlwind of quotes about family, honor and the eerie absence of Mama Corleone.

One sergeant said: "A man who doesn't spend time with his family can never be a real man."

Another sergeant answered: "You sonofabitch, do you know who I am?

I'm Moe Greene."

In the early morning they marched through the wet streets like a marching band without instruments. They beat their chests numb and smiled and recited internally to the first light and to everything that would become:

"I don't like violence, Tom. *Blood is a big expense!*"

They visited the Qin Shi Huang terra cotta warriors and chariots in the Lintong District, Xi'an, Shaanxi province. One private exclaimed, "This is incredible," as another solemnly mused: "Today is the day I refuse to be part of *anyone's* funerary art collection."

They visited America's National Parks. They ate sandwiches at the Grand Canyon's rim. A private took a selfie at Zion. Naked warriors serpentined South Dakota's Badlands, fled from a park ranger and hid in trees. Yosemite Park yawned, and they outraged Wyoming and Nevada governors when they lit firecrackers in Yellowstone National Park and planted marijuana seeds in Death Valley while giggling through long-inspired verses by Manu Chao.

There was a solar eclipse and the meteorologist called it a "blood moon," and they wept, and they all prayed for more blood moons, as if doing so, would grant them end-less blood moons, and more importantly, endless nights to observe them.

They visited Disneyland. They took pictures while careening through *It's a Small World* on a small boat and wept to the utter lie of it all.

They spent a week at an all-inclusive resort in Cancún. Needless to say, war ceased, it refrained from uttering one bilious syllable for an entire week. They sang songs and drank gallons of brightly colored alcohol.

In the distance, one practiced yoga as the sunset sat on his left shoulder, and the cyan sea alit like a snowflake from the headlights of a '67 Chevy Impala.

His silhouette aroused applause from his comrades and all of them danced ecstatically.

When assigned Heraclitus by a heavily starched war cabinet member, they mooed and booed and told him he was too late with that Heraclitus hemlock because they'd already ingested Ernesto Cardenal and would design a timetable in which they could all share his beret.

They replicated Eleanor Antin's "100 Boots" by hiring a wartime photographer and a New York Times journalist to document their pursuits across the United States as they stood their empty boots in various positions.

One image captured boots picketing the Shamu tank at Sea World, and another pair, placed strategically on a deserted street next to a candle and cardboard, read: "Stop, don't shoot. This is not a war."

They chanted bumper sticker slogans on street corners like "Arms are for hugging."

At 3 AM a sleepless man looked out his bedroom window at a large moon. In the distance, he noticed a silhouette of a hundred or so figures wearing helmets, dancing and raising their rifles victoriously across the hills of a nearby park. Rubbing his eyes, the man opened his window and heard the distant howls: "Fuck your wars!"

The man joined their nocturnal revolution by removing a picture of his deceased father from a drawer and kissed it before pressing it carefully into his pillow where he'd eventually fall asleep.

In an instant, the warriors donated their camouflage to all of the impoverished regions of the world. Jackets, pants, gloves, and socks spread flatly across glass-littered lots, and from the helmet, evolved a new rain catcher.

In an instant, millions of children and their parents played soccer until nightfall amidst a large re-appropriated material of peace.

II
THESE DAYS OF CANDY

Our legs are the pistons that fire our march through life, or at night two pipes through which each previous day's dramas drain.

—John Keene

There is nothing wrong with me but life.

—Kenneth Patchen

El sueño perfecto es el que participa de la realidad y la consume.

—Rafael Pérez Estrada

Pequeñitas estrellas luminosas guiñándonos eternamente un ojo desde un lugar del universo llamado los laberintos.

—Roberto Bolaño

THESE DAYS OF CANDY

PLAYLIST IN ORDER OF APPEARANCE
Sigur Rós: "Glósóli"
Dirty Beaches: "Casino Lisboa"
Gonjasufi: "Ageing"
Salvia Palth: "I Don't Know Anyone I Am"
Brian Eno: "The Big Ship"
Twelve Hour Turn: "It's Your Move"
David Bowie: "Lady Stardust"

PROLOGUE

PLAY TRACK: "Glósóli" by Sigur Rós

Begin reciting PROLOGUE at 0:27. After concluding the PROLOGUE, the track should continue until the reader's intuition emotes: "Enough, time to move on." When the reader's intuition emotes: "Enough, time to move on," slow FADE OUT.

If you're a famous pianist and I cut off your arm, then what will you do?

I'll become a famous painter.

And if I cut off the other one, then what will you do?

Well, I'll become a famous dancer.

And if I cut off your legs, then what?

Then I'll become a famous singer.

And if I slit your throat, then what?

Once dead, my skin will become a beautiful, beautiful drum.

And what if I burn the drum?

I will become a cloud and take on any shape.

And if the cloud dissolves, what then?

I will become rain and make the grass grow.

Okay, you win. I'm going to miss you when you're gone.

If you ever feel too lonely, search for me in the magical city.

ETDB, you *are* going aren't you? Aren't you, ETDB? Aren't you? Tell me, you are, aren't you?

I don't know.

I don't *know*?

I don't know.

I don't *know*?

I mean Don Felipe's cranky, and he smells funny, Mouse Pad. Why can't he just tell us what he sees? How many times has he made these trips? I mean, Mr. Signal, are you serious? Everyone says that it's time for Don Felipe to recruit an assistant, but I don't know if I'm—if I'm, if I'm capable of—

Ahhhh…

I don't know if I can assume that responsibility, Mouse Pad. I don't know if I'm capable of anything. (ETDB drops his head and draws a widow spider in the dirt with his foot.)

Look ETDB, if you don't make this trip, you'll regret it for the rest of your short-ass life. Don Felipe is ancient, and in the very near future, as you know very well motherfucker of the motherfuckers, he won't be able to make these expeditions. You do know that.

I do—

Don't you?

I—

Don't you? Please assure me that you know that. *Please*, ETDB.

I know, Mouse Pad, but I'm not sure if I'm capable of fulfilling something so immense.

O, come on!

Why don't *you* go? You're tougher than I am! You've always been stronger!

It's not my destiny.

Whuh?

It's not my destiny, ETDB.

we are born from memory's echo

from whuh?

of echo   *of echo*   *of echo*

     of echo   *of echo*

     of echo

It's yours. And quit feeling sorry for yourself. It's pathetic. It's your time, ETDB. I always told you this minute would come.

Would come.

I AM losing the vague dread, the fear of the thing.

The thing.

Besides, I heard that once a luciérnaga makes it, Mr. Signal grants that luciérnaga ten extra days of life. Of *life*! Imagine that! What I wouldn't give for ten extra days of life!

Of life.

A steady dismay and horror seizes me and prevents me.

With ten extra days, I'd…I'd…Ay, I don't know what I'd do, but I sure would love and cherish each and every one of them.

Whuh?

I'd hug and kiss each new sunrise like a pillow blooming from the badlands. LIKE A PILLOW FILLED WITH GARDENIAS HIGH ON ANGEL DUST, ETDB!

The garden.

The garden is.

I can see them now, feel them even, I can feel them on my face (Mouse Pad Becky closes her eyes and counts theatrically.)

…1…2…3…

We don't last long, ETDB. You know that. To have the time to see how things change. To see how things evolve. Don't you want to know? What will Hard Bent Tube Sock look like in ten hours, not to mention ten days?

And if I cut off the other one what will you do?

Look at this place. It's wilting before our eyes. (Pause.) These days I've got allergies so bad I fart dust flakes.

They laugh.

Poof!

We laugh.

Poof!

Come on…

Poof!

Yes, come on!

Go on

and go!

○

Hurry up, Kid. You're already proving yourself too slow.
At the rate you travel you'll never make a full-time explorer.

O come on, Don Felipe.

How are you doing on water?

I'm doing fine. I don't drink much water.

That explains why you don't sweat much.

> *(I very much like to think that*
> *illness sometimes heals us*

I'm ok Don Felipe. Don't worry about me. I'm a minimal-
ist. It doesn't take much for me to operate this body.

Grumble. Grumble. Grumble.

Don Felipe? *Don Felipe?* Can you hear me?

Grumble. Grumble. Grumble.

I don't need much. Can you hear me, Don Felipe?

Argh!

I just don't need much is what I'm saying.

(Mimicking with his hands on his waist while shaking his ass.) *It doesn't take much to operate this body...I'm a minimalist...* Though you and that slag generation of yours can't stay off those damned cell phones you keep pasted to your beady little heads all day long.

O, c'mon, Don Felipe. This phone could save our asses!

What's that, cabrón?

My apologies, Don Felipe, but it could save us if we needed help. That's all I said.

How? Please tell me how you vapid sack of nonsense?

Well, I'm not sure. I don't even have any reception right now it seems. That's odd. Guess I spoke too soon, right Don Felipe? (ETDB chuckles.)

Figures. You new luciérnagas are all the same. Never serious. Do you want to know why I asked you to carry me on your back for thirteen kilometers?

Do I really want to know?

Because I knew that you would not question me. You're much too passive. It really is an annoying quality you possess, ETDB. I bet if I asked you to press your tongue against that cactus needle over there you'd do it without thinking twice about the possible consequences.

I wouldn't.

Yes you would, because you're a follower.

Of Life?

Of Life.

My destiny?

I'm not.

And they put handcuffs on the flowers

handcuffs if you could imagine

handcuffed flowers doing handcuffed things

blood signature for the ill-fated Madonna

a certain powdering of dead and darkened fireflies

Ah, light and shadow

but for now the moon is revealing itself like a pearl

Not to suggest him any less of a painter

beauty in shadows to guide shadow's towards beauty's end

Chiaroscuro for my equally naked heart

And Chiaroscuro will be your name

Chiaroscuro…I like it

Move into your light, Chiaroscuro

Light pours

These days

These days of candy

Then why are you here with me? Who would ever willingly subject himself to this environment if not for the simple sad fact that he is a follower?

I don't understand. You've subjected yourself to this journey *forever*.

Bah! Don't compare yourself to me. You're only here because your granny begged me to bring you along. If I had it my way, I'd never return to Hard Bent Tube Sock. Everyone, every last one of them, is a myopic nipple on the elbow of time. A single grain of sand carries more light within it.

Don Felipe?

What?

Is this journey just a plot to another cinematic cliché?

Of life?

Of life.

Whuh?

Yes.

(Stunned) How do you mean? What the hell are you mumbling about?

The old master subjects the apprentice to harassment and the like, only to teach that apprentice a profound and worldly truth—or possibly one of great metaphysical importance—in the end, perhaps, before the master exhales his final breath. (ETDB feigns death. He grasps his chest and closes his eyes.)

and we dreamed of a green night and sailed

You good for nothing maggot. You think the dangers we will encounter will abide by any script? You are one of the most foolish luciérnigas I have ever met in my life. Out of my sight!

I will not leave your sight.

And why not you cannibal? Why not you succubus of the soul?

Because I'm not a follower, and I will not follow what you say, you benign old chinche! Besides, someone needs to remind the great ancient luciérnaga to wash himself before he begins to attract too many flies.

I should tie your wings to that ocotillo bush and tap dance on your head, but I won't—

Why?

Because I would never subject my feet to such a dull surface—

of beginnings.

that hideous face of yours could burn a hole through a towel. (Don Felipe laughs, obviously enjoying the banter) Very well, follow me along the path toward the Great Mr. Signal.

PLAY TRACK: "Casino Lisboa" by Dirty Beaches. Begin reciting at 0:49.

Imagine.

Imagine what?

(Hiccup)

Imagine.

I'm imagining what?

Life gone like a long gone light parade

Don't start that! Please stop!

(Hiccup)

Your mama's blood course final

Torrential cuerpo leakage

Gong gong gone

No more! Stop!

Mid-air horizon life-flight crash

Your papa's red vita escape

Sans spir

(Hiccup)

Quit it!

Lifeless lookie loo

(Hiccup)

Quit it!

Lifeless lookie loo

(Hiccup)

Lifeless lookie loo

(Hiccup)

Finito

(Hiccup)

Vanished

Out

ABRUPT FADE OUT 1:58

○

Wake up, Lucíernega, you're only dreaming. Remember, we are never so vulnerable as when we love.

Now roar your terrible ocean roar: *ssshhhhhhhhh*

○

Mouse Pad, if I had it my way I'd plant a whole batch of pretty little flowers while sleepwalking in a dream-drunken jardín. I'd plant irises and irises and irises again.

Okay…

And when morning arrived I'd be surprised. I'd be surprised every time as if it were the first time. O yes and yes, such a greatly tilted reverie, O yes and yes and yes. And I'd be the one to pick them, and to arrange them, and to place them beneath every luciernaga's head like a tiny pillow of fragrant dreams.

Mouse Pad Becky: Cheeee-zZY!

○

I've seen horrors,

Say what?

I've seen horrors,

Say what?

horrors that you've seen. But you have no right to call me a murderer. You have a right to kill me. You have a right to do that, but you have no right to judge me. It's impossible for words to describe what is necessary to those who do not know what horror means.

....Horror. Horror has a face...And you must make a friend of horror. Horror and moral terror are your friends. If they are not then they are enemies to be feared. They are truly enemies.

What do you think of that kid? You a Brando fan? You gotta know *Apocalypse Now*, don't you now?

No.

Ok, ok, ok, whatevs, you just don't know what you're missing, and I'll just have to accept that. Brando's a genius, you know. If I could choose some other pursuit, I'd choose acting. I'm not much of an actor, though, because I'm a horrible liar, and what seems necessary to me for an actor's repertoire is the ability to transform glass into diamond with the tip of a lying tongue. How does that sound? Sometimes I'm bewitched by these daydreams of mine.

Uhh.

So the old luciérnaga brought you here to see Mr. Signal. Where is he?

Disintegration.

He didn't make it. Disintegration sure is an awful choice of words by the way. Why do luciérnagas have to insist on calling "it" disintegration? That's so bleak. So bleak indeed.

I don't know. It's always been called that.

○

How long will our kind exist, Mouse Pad?

What is that you say?

How long will we exist? How long before it's all over?

Mmmm...I had a dream, ETDB, Mmmm...about the end of us, Mmmm...and it didn't look good, Uh-uh. Mmmm...our water evaporates, and we're all left holding cellular phones trying to make the one call that will save us. But the numbers are always wrong, they're always wrong, ETDB. It's *horrible*.

I don't want to think about it anymore. (Mouse Pad Becky turns away from ETDB.) But, remember, these are only my dreams ETDB. My dreams.

○

And since it's always been called that we must continue doing so, right?

I guess. Who AM I to change it?

Who AM I to change it, he says. That's exactly the question you should be asking yourself. And you know what, I'm looking forward to the answer. What's your name?

Elias the Doom Boy.

Wow, that name of yours says it all. Think about this quote, young Elias the Doom Boy: "Woe to the man whose heart has not learned while young to hope, to love – and to put its trust in life." You like? It's not mine, but this time I won't tell you whose it is.

…no?…maybe? Wait a minute—

Hold it there.

What? What do you mean?

Mr. Signal can do a lot of things, an unbelievable amount of things, but to wait a minute, Mr. Signal cannot do.

tears mourning separation forever

tears aligned skyward

night's tears, when vitreous tattoos must land on sleeping faces

O

O, just see for yourself.

I'm unaware.

It's Vonnegut, the lighthouse.

Poor baby, how you must have suffered to have such weird thoughts.

sigh

luciferin falls above the warring corridors

100,000 fireflies across the sky

Let us wish to those chatty poets tonight

I don't understand.

Because we're an ineffable architecture of love! And in it!

To really be?

Then be it! Be hopelessly so!

O balloon yourself some love. With love we rise.

```
            t
        h       h
      e           e
```

v   v
i   i
s

i
o
n

t
h   h
e   e
v   v
i   i
s

i
o
n

t
h   h
e   e
v   v
i   i
s

i

o

n

Dear Radio Mind,

I'm afraid of the dark without you close to me.

Soft light on soft flesh

our supper is plain

but we are very wonderful

Oye, niño, think about what you're doing before you make a bigger mess. Stop daydreaming!

I got it, Don Felipe. Don't worry about me. Just worry about the universe of us, I think.

and if the cloud dissolves?

#andhowwesurvived

#andnowwesurvive

#thegreathissofwaves

#thatsoftfragilefulllight

#yoursongalovelylightssinginguntoitself

it's so beautiful when we can suddenly look up and survive

○

The sun looks angry today. The ripraps are watching, and they must be extra angry.

Don Felipe, when we reach Mr. Signal, do you think I will acquire longevity? I don't need immortality. I just want to live longer. A bit longer. (ETDB shows 'a bit longer' with his thumb and index finger.) Mouse Pad Becky told me that if someone's lucky enough to make it to the top, that lucíernaga is granted ten more days of life. Is this true?

Mouse Pad Becky told you that, eh? What else did she tell you about Mr. Signal? ETDB, tell me NOW—

○

O, calm down ETDB, quit being so melodramatic, and don't you listen to Software Soft Lucas. His mushroom grubbing inspires those ridiculous hallucinations. ETDB, of all of the luciérnagas to listen to in Hard Bent Tube Sock, you chose Software Soft Lucas? Come on! You know better than that.

But Software Soft Lucas is a seer! At least that's what his brother says. At least that's what the Academy of Chamois Faces says! His reputation and visions have been canonized, so who are we to question?

Do you want to know what I think of Software Soft Lucas? Fuck Software Soft Lucas and fuck the Academy of Chamois Faces. Mira, ETDB, Software Soft Lucas thinks he's some kind of mystic, just like everyone else thinks he is in Hard Bent Tube Sock. This is the chance you must consider. Don Felipe is a vessel. He's experienced and gained his knowledge journeying, Luciérnaga, unlike the dummies in the Academy of Chamois Faces burying their faces in inky parchments hour after hour. Don Felipe can deliver you to the knowledge, ETDB—you know that. Or else Don Felipe is just full of shit. And if he is just full of shit, imagine! Everything we've ever believed and hoped for—(pauses) is full of shit.

Do you think he's full of shit, Mouse Pad?

Well, he looks like shit, that's for sure.

A brief pause then both luciérnagas burst into laughter. After a few seconds, Elias the Doom Boy regains his wits to say:

○

I cannot stop thinking of my parents. I often wonder if I'll see them when I—

Enter Disintegration?

Yes.

So why are you here for a quote on longevity? The asking price may be too much for a little luciérnaga like you.

Why do you support the ripraps?

(Surprised.) What?

Why do you support the ripraps?

I do not support what they do. As a matter of fact, I think they're repulsive, but I know that they are simply carrying out their nature. I cannot judge them.

Do you judge us?

Of course not. Here, eat a donut with me.

I can't.

Why? Everyone likes donuts.

Sugar will kill me.

Sugar will kill you? My goodness, Elias the Doom Boy, you continue to live up to your name by the second. Would you like some water?

No, I'm ok.

Because you're a minimalist. So tell you what, let's think about why you're here. What will ten extra days mean to you?

I'm not sure I want them anymore.

I know that, but let's pretend. What would you do?

I'd build a future without ripraps. I'd sweep away all

borders with a great big giant broom even if it meant using all ten days.

Wow, you're an ambitious little luciérnaga. How do you think the ripraps would feel about that?

The ripraps wouldn't like it, I'm sure. But that's what's coming to them, Mr. Signal.

And what if there was a little riprap, the exact same age as you are now, saddened by this sudden apocalypse, if you will? And what if he journeyed to me, asking the same thing as you, to wipe all of the luciérnagas off the face of the earth because one little luciérnaga wished his loved ones away?

I get what you're saying, but the ripraps are unjust and violent creatures, Mr. Signal. I watched them murder an innocent living being in the desert. Their brutality is measured and deliberate cruelty.

According to whom, Elias the Doom Boy?

According to the laws of the living, Mr. Signal.

And those laws are?

That we are all equal. All life is precious.

All life is pretext?

No, all life is precious.

All life is pre-fixed.

Nevermind. All life is.

Ah. I see.

PLAY TRACK: "It's Your Move" by Twelve-Hour Turn. Begin reading at 0:36. Continue to repeat the reading of this section until FADE OUT 2:14.

Run ETDB.

I'm running.

They're after you.

I know.

They want to kill you.

I know.

Run.

I'm running.

Fly away.

I can't.

Disappear.

I won't disappear.

O sweet heroin.

Do you?

Invent another language.

Whuh?

You are beautiful. You are beautiful when you are awake.

When?

Now.

END TRACK

○

Sawfish Twin #1

Hey Mouse Pad Becky, we heard your little boyfriend
ETDB went to see Mr. Signal. Is it true?

Sawfish Twin #2

Hey Mouse Pad Becky, we heard your little boyfriend ETDB went to see Mr. Signal. Is it true?

Mouse Pad Becky

Why can't you two just gag on your bad breath like everyone else has to do when you're around?

The Sawfish Twins look at one another and smile mischievously. They shrug and continue their line of questioning.

Sawfish Twin #1

Yeah, we heard that Don Felipe is going to die, and that he only took ETDB with him to bury his elytra at the illustrious feet of Mr. Signal. That is, Mouse Pad, if there is even a Mr. Signal.

Sawfish Twin #2

Yeah, we heard that Don Felipe is going to die, and that he only took ETDB with him to bury his elytra at the illustrious feet of Mr. Signal. That is, Mouse Pad, if there is even a Mr. Signal.

The twins giggle, and then recompose themselves by covering their mouths and straightening their bodies, rigid spears aiming for the sun.

Mouse Pad Becky

You're both crazy. Both of you should be strung to the ankles of a defecating ostrich for claiming such things. When was the last time you even spoke with Don Felipe?

Sawfish Twin #1

Never.

Sawfish Twin #2

Never.

Mouse Pad Becky

That's right, because he hates you and believes that you two are toxic. You two do nothing but instigate fights, gossip, and stink up every corner of Hard Bent Tube Sock that you inhabit. So why don't you do us all a favor and fly away somewhere on the other side of the day?

Feigning hurtfulness, the Sawfish Twins, hold their hearts. Their lips quiver, and their eyes begin to well. Then they both pause and look at one another, and with a wicked and sinister disposition that works itself across their faces like an oncoming tsunami, the twins begin the assault.

Sawfish Twin #1 & Sawfish #2 in unison

The problem with you, Mouse Pad Asshole, is the same problem that everyone in this dump has. It's that you all cannot accept the truth. You all hang onto those short minutes of life that have been granted to you, believing that you will somehow find something that will offer eternal life. You are all pitifulGoing on and on with your Mr. Signal this and Mr. Signal that. You really think there's a Mr. Signal, some superhero that can heal eternally, reject evil, and offer paradise? What about the ripraps? How many have been de-limbed by those vile creatures for so long without one consequence? What about your friend Gigabyte? What about Lourdes? How heavy was her head, Mouse Pad Asshole, when you buried it? But you know what, you are the most pathetic of them all, because you hang on to that façade. Yes, you know what we mean. You pretend to be optimistic, though you know this is all a hopeless charade, don't you? It's written all over your greasy little face. You know that Don Felipe is selling out ETDB as we speak. You know that crazy old luciérnaga is walking him straight into disaster. You know he put you up to it to convince your little sweetheart that he should go. You didn't think you could keep it a secret, did you? Your aunt Oat cannot keep secrets, little one. Her mouth's a leaky faucet, just like your intentions.

Mouse Pad Becky drops her head.

○

Atone for the misery you shed.

I don't understand.

I'm a mouth with your laughter trapped in me.

A void parade. A garbage chute tripa-inching struggle.

I live through you, Mouse Pad Becky.

And I live through you, ETDB.

Consider the march of time, the lengthening of whiskers.

I approach the windowsill with grace.

We, adored by the sun.

We, adored by the moon.

You intrepid giver of self.

Behave.

I run run run run run run run away.

OH OH OH Psychokiller!

Help is on the way.

Why do we keep shrieking?

We should be whispering all the time

when we mean soft things.

○

PLAY TRACK: "Ageing" by Gonjsufi

And so Elias the Doom Boy and Don Felipe trekked
through the multi-chambered heart,

grated by the sun. Ants nearly his size attacked. Don Felipe
weakened. His walking stick faltered

upon several ascents. He stumbled and tripped. But with a
stubborn mind, he cursed Elias the Doom Boy whenev-
er the lucíernaga attempted to

assist him. Elias the Doom Boy watched Don Felipe's eyes
deepen, sinking into his skull just like Cuckoo Cantata's
did during the last

minutes of her life. ETDB's worries increased.

END TRACK.

If you ever feel lonely, search for me in the magical city.

○

Why does he have to be that way? I'm so confused by everything these days. Why are we even here? Why do the ripraps have to be so resistant? Imagine if we could all visit Mr. Signal, all of us, Mouse Pad. (ETDB pauses.) Sometimes Disintegration seems like a reasonable conclusion.

ETDB, I know you don't mean that. And now I'm going to pretend that I didn't even hear it, ok? (Mouse Pad Becky closes her eyes and spins, humming a beautiful little song she learned from her great, great, great nana, Missile Pop.)

You've washed your superhero towel, yes?

Mama Flesh and Bone helped me wash and fold my superhero towel.

Good.

My towel is clean. Would you like to smell it?

Mouse Pad Becky smiles and kisses Elias the Doom Boy's forehead.

Into the furious lashing of the tides

He's gravity's protest margin.

His skin a thousand pecking-kisses-land.

His wings, picket signs above the churning fray.

INTERLUDE: DANCE OF THE SUPERHERO TOWEL

PLAY TRACK: "I Don't Know Anyone I Am" by Salvia Palth. Song should conclude at 2:03.

ETDB's superhero towel inches slowly out of his rucksack. It yawns. It shakes itself awake after a long day's nap. The superhero towel rises carefully and stretches. It jumps half-heartedly three times, then takes flight, lifting itself into the embraces of the star-trashed night.

The towel lashes through the air in long, graceful sweeps somersaulting and tumbling. It laughs and sighs. It snaps hard when changing direction:

Shoooosh Swiiiisssshhh Saaaaassss

The moon smiles its immense affirmation, widening, infectious.

Fireflies suddenly lift themselves from the desert's expanses to join the towel in a nocturnal choreography of inspired glitter, a bright sky that becomes an undulating sequins river.

Shoooosh Swiiiissshhh Saaaaassss

ETDB and Don Felipe sleep as the song concludes and the superhero towel runs one last pass, hovering gently over ETDB and Don Felipe before tucking itself quietly back into the rucksack.

END TRACK.

○

I will become rain and make the grass grow.

For we are such stuff that dreams are made of

For whom?

and our little life, rounded with sleep.

For whom?

Soft light on soft flesh

Girl with the radio mind / moon's oar dipped into dream

O these days of candy

○

Don Felipe, why is Mr. Signal so important to us? Don Felipe, are you sure we're not living a cliché?

Turn off your light, Luciérnaga!

○

I see. But what if I told you Don Felipe did not enter Disintegration, but that he is here alive and well with me? What if I told you, Elias the Doom Boy, that Don Felipe has returned to his childhood, that he no longer ails, aches or…give me another verb that starts with an "a."

Awaits.

Oh, good one. Profound, little luciérnaga, that's profound.

What if I told you he ate one of these donuts and extended his life by returning to the beginning?

I began to feel this way when I learned of my parents' death.

You felt those itchy, little feelings long before you were ever born, Luciérnaga. When Don Felipe called you the Chosen One on the Lost River, he was not lying to you.

I don't understand.

○

PLAY TRACK: "The Big Ship" by Brian Eno. The reading's pace should be accelerated.

Elias the Doom Boy and Don Felipe row down the Lost River on an ancient banana leaf. Don Felipe removes a tripod and projector from his rucksack and casts a film against the thick mist that acts like a backdrop. Don Felipe orders Elias the Doom Boy to cover his ears with his hands and to focus only on the images projected. In the periphery are the Moaning Malevolents who reek of sulfur and burnt flesh, reaching into the banana leaf, their water-bloated arms swing, their hands grab. Tears stream from ETDB's eyes.

The image of a small lamb is suddenly projected. Mouse Pad Becky emerges from the periphery and follows the small woolen creature. She is enlarged, measuring up to the lamb. She hugs the animal and closes her eyes. She kisses the top of its head. She waves at ETDB and winks, but the mist that billows out in large thick gusts soon absorbs her, and she vanishes. ETDB wipes rainwater from his face. Scenes reminiscent of Dante's *Inferno* and Hieronymous Bosch. The film is about the reversing of time. It's about the order of the world collapsing upon itself in stop motion, everything at once occurring simultaneously, until there is nothing left but a wink, and then, only to begin again.

The Moaning Malevolents bellow. They gurgle ETDB's name. A frightening chorus of deranged whispers soar past his ears like bats. The stench of flatulence. Blood. Mud clots are flung at the makeshift raft. Stones hit Don Felipe's head and back. Don Felipe is bleeding from his nose and ears. EDTB is crying as he watches images of his parents emerge from the darkness, who fly acrobatically before him. EDTB's mother pauses. She smiles and points at his father who spells out ETDB's nickname with the illuminated residue of his flight pattern. Echo Echo it reads. Echo Echo. ETDB reaches toward them as both he and Don Felipe are pounded by mud, spit, excrement, river water and tugged by the Moaning Malevolents. Then ETDB's parents wave and disappear, and the lamb returns and bends toward him as if inviting ETDB to pet it, OR, perhaps, to simply bow to a new king. More lambs. Lambs in all directions. White. Shiny. Silver. The tripod nearly falls over. Don Felipe hollers at ETDB to keep watching, Whatever you do, Luiérnaga, keep watching, and whatever you do keep your light dim otherwise THEY will see us. We cannot be seen, Lucíernaga! Keep looking at the images on the screen. Ignore what is around you! Listen only to your heart, Lucíernaga!

But it's too much, Don Felipe! I'm losing my strength!

Keep watching! Stay focused, you are now one of the chosen ones and they know it! They certainly know it, Lucíernaga! We ALL certainly know it…

Then it is over. ETDB collapses. Darkness.

(ETDB wakes up on a small hammock that Don Felipe constructed for him out of long weeds and riverbank mud.)

Go to bed, boy.

Don Felipe, what waits for us beyond the stars?

Sleep, boy.

Is there anything after this, Don Felipe?

All there ever is, is more sleep, Boy.

Goodnight, Don Felipe.

Good night, Lucíernaga.

Don Felipe?

Hard Bent Tube Sock is where they live and where they love.

but I'll give no more presents to mares

I was one—with a sugar lamb's eye I gazed

I too AM an angel

Motherfucker *right!*

Motherfucker *fight!*

◯

And remember that sometimes that is a good thing. Just think of yourself as a very important piece of the puzzle.

Like puzzle pieces we are all—

There's that phrase you mentioned earlier.

But what can I do?

I'll tell you what. I AM going to give you the opportunity to view everything. Come on, say it with me: everything.

Everything.

Everything that has ever existed. Everything that exists now. And everything that will exist in the future.

I don't understand.

Never odd or even.

Whuh?

Allí trota la tortilla.

Whuh?

Palindromes, silly. Front/Words-Back/Words

I—

Dog, as a devil deified, lived as a god.

To see everything?

There's everything to see. Enough. You will visit my basement, walk down stairs past two restroom doors where you will find a third door on the left. That door will open. There you will find what you are looking for. A descendant of yours named Borges constructed an Aleph and that is where it remains. It's quite a show. No one has ever experienced it besides Borges himself—and yours truly, of course.

Don Felipe?

Not even Don Felipe. He never asked the right questions. So if you're interested, grab those goggles, Walkman, and cassette tape and head below if you wish to peek.

Ok.

Do you really want to do it? You might not like what you see?

I'm ready.

There's one catch, though.

What is that?

You may never return. As the missing piece, you will fasten yourself into the mix in order to complete the—

Puzzle?

The puzzle. You think of your parents often, yes?

I do.

○

So you're saying it's true?

Did I say that? Did you hear those words come from my mouth? Let's start walking. We have a long day ahead of us. And get this extra life out of your head! What's the matter with you? False hope kills more completely than fly swatters. As a matter of fact, it spreads like a virus, so tighten your mouth, boy.

Mouse Pad Becky also mentioned that those who are lucky enough to return from the mountain reek of hibiscus in their sleep. Or lavender? Or were they gardenias? Anyway, she said the body begins to smell like a beautiful flower, instead of like the horrendous chemicals we reek of, especially you, Don Felipe.

Has Mouse Pad Becky ever reached Mr. Signal? Do I smell like a damn flower? Smell this. Don Felipe puts his foot in ETDB's face.

Geez, Don Felipe. You smell rotten.

Then why would you listen to a story like that?

These days of candy.

O

Can you tell me more about Mr. Signal, Don Felipe?

No, I cannot. We are approaching the Lost River now. Mira, Elias the Doom Boy, no matter how thirsty you are, you cannot drink the water from the river.

The chorus of Moaning Malevolents?

The chorus of Moaning Malevolents.

○

Once dead my skin will become a beautiful, beautiful drum.

○

And your parents think of you.

What will happen to me if I decide to see the Aleph?

I'll let Borges tell you. Let me just say, that you are the one who can—

I don't understand.

Luciérnaga, it's time for Mr. Signal to return to his donut duties. If you choose to go, you have chosen well. If you don't, you have chosen well. You know the directions to both entrance and exit. In the end, they are synonymous;

they are just the same.

Mr. Signal disappears. ETDB remains.

Heat lamps buzz.

 to the deserts built on the hill   be still

 here, we transfer our heat

 for fun cities. Salvation is a mountain.

 …*ssshhhhhhhhh*

Don't be a draught-horse, work with pleasure only.

WE'VE BEEN EXPECTING YOU, SAYS GRONK, WITHOUT DISRUPTING THE RHYTHM OF HIS PAINTBRUSH.

PEOPLE LIKE TO HOLD ONTO LIFE IN MANY WAYS, BUT EVERYTHING IS TRANSITORY. THIS IS IT, RIGHT NOW.

AND LOVE IT?

TRUCHA PORQUE NO HAY TIEMPO

TAKE YOUR MEMORY WITH YOU. YOU OWN MEMORY BY TAKING IT INSIDE YOU AT A PARTICULAR MOMENT IN TIME.

If in fine fettle, write.

IT RAINS IN HARD BENT TUBE SOCK.

IT'S KIND OF LIKE OUR JOURNEYS, THOSE WE TAKE IN LIFE, THE DIFFERENT THINGS THAT WE BUMP INTO, OR HUMMINGBIRDS FLYING AROUND IN THE STUDIO.

BEAUTY TO ME IS WHEN YOU SHOW SOMETHING TO SOMEONE THAT THEY'VE NEVER SEEN BEFORE.

When you can't create, work.

THE PAINTERS WORK.

Don't be nervous. Work calmly, joyously, recklessly on whatever is at hand.

PAINTERS WORK.

& sometimes I wonder where I'll be

when swordfish swim & the private boat dips its oars

In him, the belly is a bandage of glory

That's not what I'm waiting for. That's not what I'm look-
ing for.

○

Then why go? Why risk your life for such a trip that pays
back nothing?

Stop! Shut your mouth.

Elias the Doom Boy bumps into Don Felipe before halting.

You see over there, up on that ridge?

(Shading his eyes with his wing.) I don't see any—.

Don't move.

○

A neon glow at the top of the mountain. When ETDB
reaches the summit, he finds a Winchell's Donut House,
and a hefty employee setting trays of donuts in a display
case for the day.

○

Dream good dreams, he said. After all, that is all there ever is, he said.

○

I feel like I know what to do when it arrives

the wreckage

Where does it come from do you think?

the glow.

That predisposition to live a calm life as light diminishes to a wink.

Mama? Papa? Is there anybody out there?

Dear Mouse Pad,

The sky seems a million times larger out here than at Hard Bent Tube Sock. I've seen so much. Don Felipe is doing well enough. He's patient with me. I'm afraid, Mouse Pad, but I know this is something I have to complete. I promise to be back soon. We'll help everyone at Hard Bent Tube Sock. We will. Goodbye friend.

ETDB erases his letter in the sand with his foot. He pulls out his superhero towel and inspects it, slowly passing its fabric and stitching with the palm of his hand. ETDB smells it. It reminds him of his mother.

○

But you're Mr. Signal.

That is correct.

And you can't stop time?

Not even for a minute.

I love life, Mr. Signal.

Sure you do. And that's why you've come to receive more of it, right?

I guess.

You guess? Well, do you or don't you?

I do and I don't.

Okay, you win. I'm going to miss you when you're gone.

#achoiceismade

ETDB descends the staircase that leads to the basement. The smell of sugar and dough is overwhelming. He plugs his nose. ETDB walks past two bathroom doors to his right and sees the final door on his left. The door opens on cue and a shaft of light blasts through and widens against the wall. ETDB pulls his goggles and headphones from his rucksack just as instructed by Mr. Signal. He takes a deep breath. ETDB thinks of his parents. He thinks of Mama Flesh and Bone. He thinks of Mouse Pad Becky. He thinks of Don Felipe. He thinks of all of the lucíernagas who remain at Hard Bent Tube Sock. Then he hears Mr. Signal's voice from a speaker above him. "Now you have thought of them and they will all be fine, Lucíernaga. Elias the Doom Boy, doomed in your hands we are surely not. Your journey has just begun." Elias the Doom Boy inserts the small tape in the tape deck and pushes play. The first bar of David Bowie's "Lady Stardust" sounds as the lucíernaga steps into the light:

Play Track: "Lady Stardust" by David Bowie

One step forward.

Two steps.

Three steps.

Four steps.

Light pours over ETDB as he enters.

The door shuts behind him.

The basement hallway remains still. An overhead lamp flickers several times then extinguishes forever.

○

And your superhero underwear?

Mama Flesh and Bone helped me wash and fold my superhero underwear.

Mouse Pad Becky and ETDB embrace. Mouse Pad Becky pinches ETDB's cheek before retreating to camp. ETDB remains. He stares at the sun until a feeling suddenly inspires him to wave; like a goodbye, perhaps, to a very old friend.

THE END

III

I'm like time eating ice.
After I'm done, I don't know what I ate.

—Kim Hyesoon

TEN NEW SUPERSTITIONS

1. Wear a football jersey inside out on Sundays while reciting Cesar Vallejo, Clarice Lispector, or Blaise Cendrars.

2. To improve your writing read aloud ten gossip magazines in succession and deliver vanity's *moscas* straight back to their source.

3. Contaminate the sanctity of ego worship by uncapping a coke vial of flatulence whenever you find yourself too close to its presence.

4. Escape from yourself with your mind intact then lose it at the first corner.

5. Treat your art like a spaceship and fly away.

6. For good luck clack your teeth while walking behind the ghost of a deceased poet as if biting into its *nalgas* mid-air.

7. Simmer a large pot of books for three hours then strain them of their impurities and insistence upon dull logic.

8. Sit down and write the most vulgar poetry ever conceived of.

9. Break down the fourth wall and resurrect the theater of panic.

10. To avoid bad luck hum the first verse of the greatest poem of all time, though use discretion, because many will disagree with your choice and attempt to cut you.

THREE WORLDS

for clemente

Francesco's syntax is a neon drip technique on Earth's insufferable paper.

Paper culture fears the fire-eater.

Paper culture trembles a chalky-lipped drought.

Paper culture is an insurmountable inflammation of ink.

Francesco never says stupid things when he talks.

Francesco doesn't tell me what time his plane left for somewhere or other.

Francesco doesn't tell me how late his flight was or whether it was raining or sunny.

Francesco eats with his right hand and scratches art with his left.

Thermostats are afraid of Francesco's hands because one cannot artificially replicate the arctic immensities of his art.

There is an owl on Francesco's shoulder. A sparrow. Two thimbles cup his nipples like leather football helmets.

His art is an allegory of the sea: below, a white ship and a blonde bundle of electric bananas.

A shadow and its bowtie await the unsuspecting birdman behind the neon convenient store.

A skull nibbles on a young magician's forehead, a skull he wears for a hat.

His entire aesthetic is dedicated to disappearing the cavernous eye sockets, the mandible locked, a skull with no ears to bear the young magician's pleas.

All art results in failure.

The zebra, tiger, elephant, lion and giraffe stand gracefully on the tips of Francesco's fingers, an animal for each digit. "Why the giraffe chose my thumb, I will never know," he says. The artist shakes his head in wonderment.

Francesco gazes at the nearby mountain and combs its surface with his amphibious eyes as if searching for the vulture that will someday feed on his earlobe.

Francesco brought back a seashell from the Mediterranean belly, and like a campaign button, pinned it to the Italian afternoon.

Seashell water spilled over my bare feet, and I was six-years-old again.

Twelve sheets of handmade Pondicherry paper, joined by cotton strips.

Pigment on cloth.

A row of teeth exits a lover's mouth strung from a taut line of floss as if tethered to the irreparable lie he thought buried forever in the subconscious of addiction.

Pigment on cloth.

Francesco holds a lit candle above his head and levitates like a sandaled monk high on angel dust.

Who are you, Francesco, strange carrot in the hand of the creator?

Francesco's watercolor "Skin" inspired nightmares for weeks.

You remember your neighbor, the old drunk stabbed by his stepson, story you shared with Francesco days after while organizing brushes.

Is this the true source of "Skin?"

Your neighbor was a walking punch bowl, and you couldn't think of anything but your erection.

Is that strange, you asked Francesco?   Francesco said it was, and now you have this picture between you.

Books are the secret utterances of visionary clowns undressed in their inner locker rooms.

Francesco told me that the spiders of Jamaica came to greet him all dressed up in a procession because he had done a painting of a spider who was the king of the island.

with lines by E Ettore Sottsass

AND THE DINOSAURS
RAN UNCOLLECTED

like a band of covetous men

destroying their nostrils with run

EMERSON'S LAMENT

Nonetheless, I've become a professional cartographer. I work for the government. More specifically, I work for the military. My maps could locate an early Egyptian lip balm on the edges of the Manzala Lake if one needed to be recovered. Most recently, the US Navy used my maps to capture a runaway firefly that escaped from a research facility in San Diego, California. Authorities caught up to the tiring insect thirty-seven and a half miles into the Pacific and returned it to service the next day despite its exhaustion, despite its refusal to offer light. It died one week later but *that* is another story. My work with map-making was adopted by Roger L. Easton during his earliest developments of the Global Positioning System. Since then, one might say I've become a legend within the community. I've arm-wrestled the elusiveness of fugitive discoveries and won. I am, as Emerson once wrote, "the transparent eyeball. I AM nothing; I see all."

QUAKE

An angel's fall is a direction…Harmony, terrible harmony, is our only prior destiny.

—Clarice Lispector

The angels wanna wear my red shoes.

—Elvis Costello

The angel of Marlboro Smoke Road emerged from its coral reef like a small, ornate necktie.

My neighbor insists: "These hooligans might very well be members of a twenty-first century cavalry fixed on intergalactic expansion."

The angels are giggling and odorous. So beautiful, they reek of mead.

José's front door was strong-armed by a rambunctious mob of rollerblading angels insistent upon skating unhindered through his living room.

You hear them laughing at three o'clock in the morning threatening cyanide pills stamped with hairy insignias in your morning coffee.

The angels have stolen every light bulb in her home and now she is without light.

My heart sank when I discovered angels were filled with helium.

Shattered I schooed away the moon with a tabloid and submerged myself neck-deep in its milky lachrymation.

The angels have painted their flowered faces obsidian while a telluric hunger flashes beneath their tongues.

A tobacco-toothed angel scraped its bloody gums with a razor blade. There is an infinite rainforest embroidered on its cape encircled by a microscopic neon peephole.

The angels flour-footed all over my favorite kitchen mural.

Thirty-four thousand angels wheelbarrowed inflation.

When I grow weary I can no longer resist the temptation to count the missing plates emptied from my cupboards, all because of some drunken angel's fondness for Frisbee.

In bed broken verses bleed over my bare feet like the head of a decapitated carousel horse planted by two-bit cinema gangsters.

Pretending to sleep I relish the news of a new rising lord intent on withdrawing its troops.

HAIKU WITH HASHTAG

when my sobriety
is an overheated radiator
begging clouds for rain

#atleastistillhavemywingsma

IV

SHOVEL

1

The Saddened Man researches Craigslist and finds a small puppy. It's eight weeks old and it weighs just over a pound. The Saddened Man finds the puppy's brown fur appealing, which is rare these days, he thinks, to find anything at all appealing. The saddened man enlarges the puppy's image and outlines the animal's small body with his fingertip on the screen. He reads: "eight week old maltipoo. distemper shots."

The Saddened Man sends the owner a message: "What is a Maltipoo exactly? Does it have an exotic origin? Are Maltipoo's happy? For goddsakes are they happy?"

The Saddened Man walks out of his apartment and into the courtyard to smoke a cigarette. He wonders if a puppy could alleviate the sadness that is eating him away, a sadness that vibrates in his belly and devours all of his food, all of his water, all of his light.

2

The Saddened Man doesn't do much these days. His family no longer speaks to him. His Only Friend moved to Nebraska to take over her deceased mother's home after two years of dragging her feet, claimed her sister. The Saddened Man asked his Only Friend to list ten reasons why she'd ever want to move to Nebraska. The Saddened Man's Only Friend could only think of two: her mother's home and corn. She always loved corn, though she wasn't certain if farmers in Nebraska even grew it anymore.

The Saddened Man tried to convince his Only Friend to stay, but his Only Friend said that the opportunity to live without worrying about rent was too great to refuse.

3

At the Greyhound bus station, The Saddened Man gave his only friend a hug and said, "We'll always have Skype, I guess." His Only Friend nodded and said, "Take care of yourself. Keep yourself busy. Why don't you get yourself a pet? That will help with the loneliness. Probably won't be much of a Scrabble player, but it'll sure get you through the dead days."

The Saddened Man struggled to smile, always a problem for him, though his lips and mouth gestured a slight indication of relief from this difficult moment. "The way you play Scrabble, the pet might be tougher competition," he said.

4

Days go by, and The Saddened Man hasn't heard from the dog's owner via Craigslist. The Saddened Man remains hopeful and begins to compose a list of names because he wants to be prepared if he's notified. He tears out a piece of spiral bound notebook paper and folds it in half, vertically numbering the column one to fifteen just like he did for his elementary school spelling tests. The puppy's names are both male and female, and several ungendered, because he's not quite sure what the puppy's gender is. Honestly, he thinks, I don't know what gender means.

1. Ophelia
2. Persephone
3. Hamlet
4. KW
5. Claire
6. Douglas
7. Artax
8.

9.

10.

11.

12.

13.

14.

15.

5

After six days, The Saddened Man receives an email from the puppy's owner. He says that it's still available, though he doesn't know how much longer he'll have it because many have expressed interest. **HE'S A CUTE PUPPY**, the owner types in bold capital letters, and The Saddened Man's heart accelerates and his stomach gurgles wide and all-encompassing. The Saddened Man steps away from his laptop and considers the message, the possibilities, the challenges, the potential heartache. What if the dog hates him? What if the dog eats everything in the house? What if the dog depletes his fixed income? The Saddened Man draws a Venn diagram, the only thing he learned how to draw in high school.

6

(The Saddened Man always loved Venn Diagrams. They made sense to him. Overused, yes, but they made sense to him. To amuse himself in class he'd sometimes draw nipples on the two circles that constructed the chart, but when it was time to submit them for credit, he'd vigorously erase them or draw something over the nipples to disguise his perversions. The satisfaction of subversion excited him very much. Each Venn diagram he drew was a palimpsest of a young man in the process of omitting himself at the back of the class.)

7

On one circle he wrote pros, and on the other, he wrote cons. In the middle, where the two circles shared area, he wrote events that might be considered temporary. For example, a sudden illness might be temporary, like a bacterial infection that could be remedied with a brief battery of antibiotics. He considered this a temporary setback, though one that wouldn't necessarily break him emotionally or financially.

8

The Saddened Man met the puppy's owner at a McDonald's parking lot near the 74 Freeway. For some reason, the Saddened Man was nervous. Why do I feel like I'm committing a crime, he thought. He felt like everyone was watching him. He counted the cars in line at the drive-thru. There were vans, cars and trucks. He counted nine automobiles. One of them had to be a DEA agent or an undercover police officer, he thought. The van with the carpet cleaning business advertisement on its doors has to be a mobile command center. Would they accuse him of dealing drugs? He'd never done something like this before. The Saddened Man bent down and pretended to adjust his license plate. He opened the hood and stood with a concerned look on his face. But he suddenly realized that some compassionate person might stop to help and then what would he do? So he dropped the hood and crossed his arms. He stood outside his car and waited for the 2 PM drop-off. Would the puppy's owner really show up? Would he agree to release the dog to a man filled with so much apparent sadness?

The Saddened Man felt the rolled bills in his pocket with thumb and fingertips. He took the bills out every so often and counted them multiple times to remain certain that he had the exact amount for a quick and easy exchange. He kept the cash in his pocket because he didn't want to reach into his wallet in front of a stranger. The Saddened Man heard several Craigslist stories about people mugged or beaten for their money or merchandise.

9

The man with the puppies arrived. He drove a white Toyota Corolla. He had a little boy in the passenger seat. The man with the puppies stepped out of his car, shook the Saddened Man's hand and introduced himself. His name was Fabian. He opened the back door and pulled out a carrier. He quickly pulled out the puppy and let the Saddened Man hold it.

The Saddened Man held the puppy in his arms. Immediately overwhelmed, The Saddened Man felt like sobbing. He thought about faking a cough to trick Fabian into thinking he was dealing with the last remnants of a cold or something.

Fabian told The Saddened Man a little about the puppy. He's the runt of the litter, he said, but he's super energetic. This little guy is the most energetic puppy of the bunch.

The Saddened Man felt the urge to cry. He could no longer hear Fabian. He was completely bewildered by the tiny life in his arms. After a couple of minutes, Fabian asked The Saddened Man if he was going to take the puppy or not. "You're not just window-shopping, are you?" Fabian asked. "Yes. Yes," said The Saddened Man, "I will take him. I was just thinking is all." The Saddened Man took out the bills from his pocket and handed them to Fabian.

Fabian counted them. Fabian said, Thanks. He said, Enjoy the dog.

The Saddened Man heard the word enjoy and assured Fabian that he would. The Saddened Man thought about his Only Friend and wondered what she'd think about his new companion, and whether she'd be genuinely happy for him or whether it was all just a put on to make him feel better about her leaving.

10

The Saddened Man took the puppy home. Once at his apartment, he blocked the entryway that separated his dining area from his kitchen with six stacks of books. He figured that the linoleum would be the best place to wipe up the inevitable accidents. For two hours the Saddened Man sat with his new puppy, playing with him, staring at him in the eyes. He periodically checked his heartbeat with his index and middle fingers by placing them on the puppy's chest and back. The Saddened Man placed his ear to different parts of the puppy's body to ensure that there was a steady and observable measure of life. He imagined the sound of the puppy's blood coursing throughout his body.

The Saddened Man steamed rice and boiled some chicken for the puppy because he was told to transition slowly and carefully to kibble, to remain cautious of nausea. The Saddened Man was prepared to do anything, even though he hated the sight and smell of uncooked chicken.

11

That night The Saddened Man dreamed of his childhood dog, Lobo. Lobo was a German shepherd. He was the family dog for eight years until a car hit him. The Saddened Man wasn't home when the car hit Lobo. That day he was at the mall with his older cousin buying a new baseball glove. The Saddened Man never forgave himself for not being home when the car hit Lobo. The Saddened Man never used the baseball glove, and he stopped playing baseball altogether.

12

The next morning The Saddened Man walked into his kitchen and found the puppy lying motionless near the towel he left for him. Next to the puppy's rear was a very small pool of blood. The Saddened Man rushed to the puppy's side and placed his ear to its chest but there was nothing. The dog was unresponsive. The puppy's eyes were slightly open as if peering into another dimension. The Saddened Man grew frantic. He reached for his cell phone and called 911 but the dispatcher scolded him, insisting that he couldn't use emergency resources for an animal. "We are limited," the dispatcher said. "Call a vet or animal hospital," he said. "For godsakes! What's wrong with you?"

13

The Saddened Man sat next to the dead puppy for a whole hour before he decided to grab a hand shovel. The plan was to bury the puppy in the courtyard later that day. He'd do it in the middle of the night when everyone in the apartment complex was asleep. He returned to his bedroom and grabbed the small piece of jade that was given to him long ago by his cousin, Nestor. Shaped like a miniature pyramid, this would become the puppy's headstone, his plot. He'd been saving the jade pyramid in his underwear drawer for the right moment. The Saddened Man was numb and couldn't even register his own heartbeat in his body even when he attempted to hush his mind.

14

The Saddened Man would remain sad.

15

He called Fabian, but Fabian didn't answer his phone. The Saddened Man grew furious with himself with every minute that passed. He blamed himself for the puppy's death. The Saddened Man should've done more research before he decided to care for the puppy. The Saddened Man went to his closet and pulled out a black long sleeve shirt, black slacks, and black socks. He ironed them, preparing an appropriate outfit for a burial. The Saddened Man cried. Then he laughed at the absurdity of the situation. He banged his head against the couch's armrest.

16

The Saddened Man cut four guitar strings from the guitar his Only Friend gave him for his forty-seventh birthday with a pair of scissors. He left only the bottom E string and plucked it for hours at a time.

The Saddened Man created an original crossword puzzle with the same clue for every word: *This word is a synonym for sadness.*

The Saddened Man inaugurated a ritual of setting the dinner table for three and eating alone on the couch.

The Saddened Man sat in his bathtub and let the shower water wash all over him as he sobbed into his hands.

The Saddened Man repeatedly listened to "Floating Spit" by Perfume Genius.

The Saddened Man pinched the thin skin on his forearm until small beads of blood bloomed.

The Saddened Man wrote apologies to Lorca, the name he posthumously named his puppy.

17

At two in the morning The Saddened Man decided against burying Lorca in the courtyard. "That's not rest," he insisted while staring into the bathroom mirror. "Too many loud and obnoxious people live in this place. Too many damn obnoxious people everywhere!"

The Saddened Man walked one and a half miles into town. He carried Lorca, a blanket, the hand shovel and the small jade pyramid.

Dressed in black, the Saddened Man emerged from the darkness of the tree-lined street a silhouette moving through the aluminum can moonlight.

The Saddened Man would bury the puppy at his old elementary school near the swing set.

The Saddened Man would roll up his sleeves in preparation for the burial and recite the lyrics of a sad song.

The Saddened Man would utter, "This puppy will know joy," plunging his hand shovel into the earth to bury or plant his sadness again.

SANTA SANGRE

I AM disoriented from the daily blood donations extorted from the body via black and white bloodmobiles.

All that's left of me is a single drop caught somewhere between the larynx and city hall.

Whenever the court phlebotomist bites into a plum, she's reminded of me: "Time to give some more of that blood to me."

My doctor, forget about it, she or he is a disappearing act—*poof!*

In me they see an accessory of blood.

My belt buckle is stitched with red and white blood cells.

I AM a walking coagulant.

There are days when the 7-Eleven cashier resembles a needle pricing skin.

I show him my forearms and say take what you want, it won't be long before it's all gone anyway.

Governor, issue a drought—*please!*

Days pass on red velvet slippers. My bathrobe is a bandage.

My morning coffee is gauze dabbed with rubbing alcohol.

They say I AM the animal whose blood is hot and contained, blood that lubes dangerous machinery.

Tonight I want to inject this outrage into a pallid moon and watch it implode, because it witnesses the abusive language of baton and cuff but says nothing, absolutely nothing.

Lunatic! All this lunacy beneath that fat, grey shadow!

Badged pistolero: I want to fall asleep in your arms and soak your shirt.

BLUEPRINT
FOR AN AMERICAN ALLEGORY
EVENT FOR TEN ACTORS AND TWO AUDIENCE MEMBERS

A small drone, or quadcopter, eight inches in diameter. It is equipped with four miniature propellers, a GoPro camera attachment, and a blinking light. A misty aura surrounds the drone. The drone's exterior is painted the colors of the Mexican flag: green, white and red. A screen must be available and visible to the audience to see the images reported back from the drone's travels. The drone will fly over the audience throughout the entirety of the event.

The drone's operator is an eight-year-old boy who wears a Mexican luchador's mask. He wears the requisite wrestler's stretchy pants, luchador's boots, and a t-shirt with a fading logo commemorating Mexicali's centennial celebration. He wears a cape with a beautifully embroidered mosaic of the great Mil Máscaras. His mask is decorated with various bright, shimmering colors and fabrics.

A tío, tía, and six primos. The tío is forty-four years old and the tía is forty-two years old. The cousins are six boys descending from age fourteen. The age differences may vary from event to event.

An audience member monitors an EKG machine at the foot of the stage connected to the boy and periodically reports to the audience by standing up and shouting the boy's various readings.

Another EKG machine is connected to a different audience member. When the audience member connected to the EKG and the boy's EKG machines match heart activity, the audience member connected to the EKG will be instructed to shout "It's happened," though the event continues until it reaches its final scene.

Reno, Nevada. The airspace between here and there.

The boy spends most of his time in the backyard of a home he shares with his tío, tía and six primos who love him very much but who are confused by his peculiar behaviors. They think he's strange, and sometimes these evaluations seep out of their minds and can be heard vocalized behind closed doors and laughter.

His parents work at various packing sheds in California, too many towns to remember, as he waits for them in Reno, Nevada. His parents call him once a week, and the phone conversations are always tender and wearied by the great chasm of distance and yearning.

When the boy is not flying his drone, he imagines himself the great técnico at odds with all of the vile rudos of the world. He mimes elbow smashes, clotheslines, suplexes and glorious top buckle flight patterns as he leaps from a picnic table and tumbles across the grass.

These battles are immensely difficult because the rudos are just as skilled, except they possess the willingness to incorporate chairs, baseball bats, and brass knuckles into their repertoire of war.

Like Dante's *Inferno*, the boy has imagined an allegory of retribution. Figures from his life appear at the center of the ring, those who have threatened, belittled, or defied him with their iniquities. These rivals, however, are not only people, like Felipe, the bully who held him down one recess and placed his ass on the boy's face and farted, smothering his nose and mouth with the foul odor, denim and physical weight of his cruelty. Additionally, the boy combats costumed abstractions like loneliness, distance, isolation, and betrayal.

For example, the boy's toughest battle was waged against the masked embodiment of *otherness*. The match lasted an entire weekend. The arena was filled to capacity. Even his tío, tía and six primos stood dumbstruck at the sliding glass door with their palms and noses squashed against the glass. Otherness kicked and clawed. Otherness pointed its index finger at the boy's heart and shrieked. The boy shielded himself with a jade amulet then unleashed 482 wild punches that rocked otherness back three neighborhood blocks. At the match's conclusion, the boy and his archenemy remained flattened across the ring's canvas in a draw before a sudden Nevada wind whisked otherness away to fight the boy another day.

The drone flies great distances. The boy has ingeniously rigged the drone with an imaginary curandero's concoction made of herbs, Crayola shavings, tamarindo,

Tampico and Chamoy so that it can fly for an indeterminate time, like an immortal and relentless colibrí, like Earth's gravitational antithesis, like a mythological deity among an aviary of drones devoted to war, commerce and other human perversions.

The boy flies his drone over Mazatlán and into his grandparents' home. He flies it over the California packing sheds where his parents have worked, searching, his drone always arriving too late— The boy flies the drone over the U.S. elementary school that he will attend in the fall; he flies the drone over his old primaria in Mexicali; he flies the drone over wrestling arenas in Tijuana; he flies the drone over bi-national pockets of poverty and violence to prove a clear and clamorous point to myopic politicians; he rests the drone at Teotihuacán and Chapultepec park.

The drone records the eccentric wanderings in a microscopic black box, the curiosities of a young boy in a strange land archived forever.

This event will conclude on the night before the boy's first day of school in the United States. The boy's drone will land on the Arctic Svalbard archipelago. It will then be transferred swiftly to the Svalbard Global Seed Vault by a team of international scientists. And it will rest there until discovered among the depths of the meticulously catalogued *chonta defensas* by a future audience of theatergoers trying to save itself from itself.

after Sawako Nakayasu

ACKNOWLEDGMENTS

Very special thanks to Carmen Giménez Smith for your belief, support, and boundless inspiration.

To the Noemi Press staff—mil gracias for your assistance and hard work. Goodness, thank you.

Thank you to Letras Latinas, more specifically Francisco Aragón, for your and Carmen's role in launching the Noemi Press Akrilica Series—this is certainly a magical place.

Thanks to Farid Matuk for your insights and spectacular vision. I'm immensely grateful.

Thank you to Mark Leidner, Farid Matuk, Joyelle McSweeney, and John Yau for lending your words of support. I'm among your most devoted fans!

Thank you to Diana Marie Delgado for reading some early drafts of these joints to help me help them.

Big love to CantoMundo and all those who embody it.

Thank you to the *Reclaiming Our Stories* community-writing project: Khalid, Mona, Roberta, Darius, Ebony, and all of the participating writers who courageously share themselves each week. Abrazos.

I'm grateful for the support and unyielding fire exhibited by my San Diego City College colleagues and students.

Enormous thank yous to my family and friends. Mom and Dad you are my greatest mentors—*period!*

Brothers, sisters, you are giants in the circus tent of my heart.

Thank you, Luka—small, "little love dog," companion of peace and compassion.

Ah, Mandie, for *everything*—steady courage-teacher.

Thank you to the editors of the following journals for publishing some of these poems: *City Works Journal*, *The Journal Petra*, and *Vlak: Contemporary Poetics and the Arts*.

Text sampled in "These Days of Candy" include works by Fernando Arrabal, Beach House, Juan Cirerol, Joseph Conrad, Ralph Waldo Emerson, bell hooks, Alejandro Jodorowsky, Henry Miller, Frank O'Hara, Kenneth Patchen, Arthur Rimbaud, Maurice Sendak, William Shakespeare, Patti Smith, Van Gogh, Alma Luz Villanueva, and John Yau.

Other texts sampled include excerpts from *Apocalypse Now*, *Bomb Magazine*, and Wikipedia.

ABOUT THE AUTHOR

Manuel Paul López's books and chapbook include *The Yearning Feed* (2013), *1984* (2010), and *Death of a Mexican and Other Poems* (2006). He co-edited *Reclaiming Our Stories: Narratives of Identity, Resilience, and Empowerment* (2016). A CantoMundo fellow, his work has been published in *Bilingual Review*, *Denver Quarterly*, *Hanging Loose*, *Huizache*, *Puerto del Sol*, and *ZYZZYVA*, among others. His work has been supported by the San Diego Foundation's Creative Catalyst Fund. He lives in San Diego and teaches at San Diego City College.